Parental Grief

Surviving the
First Two Years

6

Steps You Can Take
to help cope with the grief
of losing your child

Donna J Luke

djL
Press

Parental Grief, Surviving the First Two Years: 6 Steps
You Can Take to help cope with the grief of losing your
child

djL
Press

an imprint of
djLuke enterprises
9712 Compadre Ln NE
Albuquerque, NM 87111

ISBN-10: 0-9977726-0-3
ISBN-13: 978-0-9977726-0-9

Contents

Introduction

Some bereaved parents come through the process of grief and mourning quite well with the support of family and friends and their marriage stays intact. But some parents end up with a double or triple whammy. Not only do they lose their child, but they lose their friends and some lose their spouse too.

I'm hoping that AWARENESS through this book can help decrease these losses and make your journey a bit easier.

Surviving the First Two Years

This book will give you some steps you can take during those first two years to work through the loss — things you need to do in the beginning like plan for the funeral and things you can do after that to work through the grief. Each chapter will include stories from people I interviewed, quotes from professionals and tips from research gleaned from reliable websites — presented in an easy to grasp format. I say "easy to grasp format" only because I know that if you are within the first two years of your child's death, you are probably still in bit of a fog and numbness, and trying to focus on these "things" isn't easy. So I did some of that work for you and have presented it here. My resources are listed in each chapter, with further details presented in an appendix.

If your child is in hospice with a life-threatening illness, as unfathomable as that is, you will have extended, quality time to spend with your child. If your child died suddenly due to an accident, suicide or SIDS/SUDS, you likely had no warning, no time to prepare and no time to say good-bye. When death occurs like that, it is so very difficult, because it happens so fast.

Either way, no parent should have to plan for their child's funeral, but sometimes they have to anyway. It's painful — you don't want to do it — but you may have to. If you find yourself in that situation, I offer you my sincere condolences. I am very sorry for your loss. Even if the funeral is over and you're still within the first few years, this book is for you. It's also for parents with a child in hospice — to help with planning.

Things You Can Do

I tend to be a "doing things" person, so I always look for the things I can DO to help a situation. In this case, I'm presenting 6 THINGS parents can DO to help cope with the grief of losing their child. There are also some tips for friends and family as they try to help the parents cope.

If you haven't planned the funeral yet, then for sure you'll want to read Chapter 1. If that event is already done, then start with Chapter 2 — Grieving and Online Support. It covers more of the mental aspects of grief, rather than "THINGS you can do" so prominent in the remaining chapters. So I've included short articles by grief experts and stories from bereaved parents to support you in your journey.

I wish you well and hope this book may be of some comfort to you.

Chapter 1

Planning the Funeral and Writing the Obituary

"The song is ended, but the melody lingers on..."
Irving Berlin

You may only have a few days to prepare. No parent gives any thought to funeral arrangements for their child . . . unless your child is in hospice.

As painful as it is to have a child in hospice care, it does provide the family with time to share some very important moments. It also allows time to pre-plan the funeral and provides the family with a support group to help them through some very difficult times.

Parents whose child dies suddenly have a different mental challenge. Some children die from SIDS or SUDS at a very young age, suddenly and for no apparent reason.[1] Some children have accidents or are in an accident. Some take their own lives. These are all unimaginable, gut-wrenching and make us feel that we've lost a part of our future we thought looked so bright.

Trying to cope with funeral plans and obituaries during this stressful and difficult time is an immense task. It takes all your strength just to get through the day, let alone complete the tasks that need to be done. Now's the time to rely on professionals to help you accomplish what you need to and the Funeral Director is vital in guiding you through the choices you need to make.

Types of Funeral Services

The **Traditional Funeral Service** typically includes the presence of the casket, with option of it being left open at the service or closed. It's common to have a visitation period, the funeral service, and then a short service at the cemetery for the immediate family and close friends. That's what we are used to attending. Especially for this type of service, be attentive to the special needs of young children.[2]

With the change in attitudes and lifestyles over the last several decades, cremations have grown from 5% in the 1960s to about 50% currently. Today more and more families are choosing cremation first and then having a

Memorial Service within a few days or a few weeks. The urn may be present or not, whichever the family chooses. These services tend to be less formal and allow family and friends to pay their respects and to find emotional support among one another.

The **Celebration of Life Service** tends to give the attendees permission to be more joyful and usually occurs several months or even a year after the death. How and where the life of the child is celebrated is up to the imagination of the parents and is a fairly open event. Everyone can take part and share their stories or memories.

Writing the Obituary

The purpose of the obituary is to notify people that your child has died and tell them when and where the service will be held. It usually also tells a brief story of your child's life. The funeral director may help you write an obituary, if you wish. They will typically publish it on their own website at no charge and will offer to publish it in a newspaper with you paying the newspaper charges.

If you are going to write the obituary yourself, be sure to contact the newspaper and/or the funeral home first to see what guidelines they may have. (The newspaper won't print the obituary until they have checked with the funeral home.)

I recently took a class on How to Write an Obituary and was pleased to hear the instructor tell us to "not make the format boring". She showed us how to make it more interesting by adding answers to questions such as "What do I want people to remember about my child?" and "What were his/her favorite activities?" Add a favorite anecdote or recollection, then sprinkle in the biographical data where it fits. Add a lead sentence or sentiment, add an ending and then pare it down by 20%.

Suggest Donation Options in the Obituary

Now is the time to mention any charities or special causes that your friends and family may wish to donate to in your child's name. If there is a special charity which resonates with you, then name it in the obituary, since this tends to be the one time when others are willing to give money to a special cause.

There are two special situations which present unique opportunities for the parents -

If Funds Are Needed for the Family

If it would be appropriate to ask for donations to the family to pay bills, see the section below about Online Obituaries and the Tributes.com website.

The Teddy Bear Option

If your child was young, consider recommending that teddy bear donations can be made through the www.TeddyBearLegacy.com website to give quality stuffed teddy bears to children in a hospital or hospice in the name of your child. A free registration on the website allows parents to choose any Children's Miracle Network hospital or a local hospice program to receive the teddy bear donations. **Be sure to include a link to the website homepage in the obituary**. The teddy bears represent the joy and love your child radiated to everyone and now your child's legacy is shared through the bears with children who need extra comfort in the hospital or hospice. These teddy bears will be cherished for months and years to come by all the children who receive them.[3]

Publishing the Obituary

If you decide to publish the obituary yourself there are now several options. You can publish it in one or more newspapers and/or you can publish it online – either on an online obituary website or on a memorial website you set up and manage yourself. All of these options have their own benefits and difficulties.

Publish in the Newspaper

One way to publish the obituary yourself is to go to www.Legacy.com, click the Newspaper tab, then click the state you want on their map. You can even choose international locations. Then choose the paper you want and click "Submit Obituary" at the bottom of the page. Obituary costs will vary with each newspaper and depend on the number of characters you include (they all count spaces and punctuation as a character). If you have access to the Microsoft Word program, you can check the character count of your notice if you highlight what you typed, then click the word count message in the bottom left corner of the computer screen once. That will bring up the Word Count pop-up. Be sure you look at the one that says "characters with spaces".

For example, the Albuquerque Journal in New Mexico charges $2.45 per line per day (a line is about 30 characters including spaces and punctuation) for the print version, with an additional $25 charge to have it available online. If you add a photo, then it costs an additional $50, as they print the pictures in color. The paragraph above is 750 characters long (starts with "You can" and ends with "pop-up"), so it would cost 750/30 = 25 lines x $2.45 = $61.25 + $25 + $50 = $136.25 plus tax to print the obituary in the paper for one day with a color photograph and to have it available online.

If your child was old enough to have lived in more than one town, you may want an obituary in the newspapers in those other towns as well. However, that can get pretty expensive. So another choice is to publish a **short version** of the obituary in the local newspaper(s) and then publish a more extensive obituary on an online site. (See the next section for details.)

Publish Online

Online obituaries are a great option in several situations:
- **IF** the cost of one or more newspaper obituaries is too much for your budget

- **IF** you want to publish a short obituary in the local paper and send visitors to a more robust version online
- **IF** you want to reach family and friends in several different cities across the country or across the globe in an affordable way
-

The Funeral Home Site —

Your Funeral Home may offer to put an obituary notice and one photo on its website for free. They will upload your information for you. It's a great service - if offered - for anyone who doesn't want to this on his own. It is not as robust as Memorial Websites discussed below, but for a number of people, this notification is sufficient.

Other Online Sites —

If you want to submit an obituary notice yourself – here are two easy-to-use websites:

FREE Online obituary — HealGrief.org

I found just one website that offers an online obituary for free. It's www.HealGrief.org, a non-profit organization out of California offering a wide variety of resources for newly bereaved families. You can choose the background image you want and upload one photo and the opportunity to tell all about the person and the services. There are no ads on the page, so it remains respectful. It also has an INVITE button to easily send a link to the site to family and friends so they can post comments and upload photos as well.

From their website: *"We offer an alternative to traditional newspaper obituaries. They are costly and time consuming. Here you can create an obituary in minutes and notify family and friends from around the world with the funeral notice."*

$20 Online obituary — Tributes.com

Tributes.com website offers obituaries for $20. (The term they use is "death notice.") It offers the notice, sharing options, unlimited text, one photo, and a guestbook for virtual candles and comments. It's unique because it is the only website I found that offers a fund-raising option to benefit the family — called Give Forward.

From their website: *"My best friend passed away and this platform gave us all the tools to set up the fundraiser for his kids the same day."* - Bryan P.

＞＞｜＜＜

Memorial Websites

If you want your family and friends anywhere to see the service information online and to be able to leave comments, stories or tributes, consider creating a memorial webpage. They try pretty hard to be user friendly and helpful if you have a question. You might want to have a short obituary notice in a newspaper (and/or on your funeral homes website) and then a longer version on your memorial webpage. Be sure to include a link to the

Memorial webpage in the newspaper and on the funeral home site. The cost for a memorial website runs anywhere from FREE to typically $50 for a lifetime of viewing. See details and distinctions in of memorial websites in Chapter 5 of this book.

Footnotes:

[1] SIDS (sudden infant death syndrome) applies when the child is 1 year or younger and SUDS (sudden unexplained death syndrome) for a child over 1 year. The Medical Examiner has no explanation for a SIDS/SUDS death.

[2] Particularly for a traditional funeral service, special care needs to be taken for young children. Experts say that as soon as possible after the death, explain to the child what has happened in a simple and direct manner and explain what will happen during the next few days. Explain funeral rituals as a way to say good-bye to their loved one. I'm told by social workers that even very young children can benefit from participating in these events, but they should not be forced to attend. Let each child choose. It may be helpful to assign them an adult "buddy" to help them if they need to leave the service or gathering.

[3] Teddy Bear Option — *"I wish I'd done this sooner."* That's what Jennifer Dugan said about the Teddy Bear Legacy. She wished the people who'd been nice enough to send her flowers could have spent that money on sending teddy bears to children in the hospital in her daughter's name.

When she worked with the funeral director in February to write the obituary, Jennifer didn't realize there was a Teddy Bear Legacy option out there. She found out about it several weeks later and went online to www.TeddyBearLegacy.com to register.

In March she set up a webpage about her daughter Megan and filled it with stories and photos. She included a section about The Teddy Bear Legacy too, and included a link so her friends and family could go to that website and donate teddy bears in Megan's name, if they wanted to.

Her goal was to try to have 640 teddy bears donated in Megan's name... because that was the number of days that she had Megan with her. She reached that number of teddy bear donations on Christmas Eve. By the anniversary of Megan's death in February, 720 teddy bears had been donated. UNM Children's Hospital in Albuquerque, New Mexico and 720 children who had been treated there all know Megan's name and the generosity of the people who donated.

NOTE :
www.TeddyBearLegacy.com is solely owned and operated by Donna J. Luke, Albuquerque, NM.

Chapter 2

Grieving and Online Support

"It has been said, 'time heals all wounds.' I do not agree.
The wounds remain. In time, the mind, protecting its
sanity, covers them with scar tissue and the pain lessens.
But it is never gone."
- *Rose Fitzgerald Kennedy*

Grief — What Is It ?

The chart on the next page shows what used to be the norm in defining the "Five Stages of Grief" model. It was developed by Elisabeth Kübler-Ross in 1969 [1] and includes denial, anger, depression, bargaining and acceptance. These steps try to explain what we may be feeling and how we will eventually learn to live without the loved one we lost. It was clear even then that the sequence was not firm and that not everyone passed through all the stages in the same order.

"NORMAL"
FUNCTIONING

RETURN TO
MEANINGFUL LIFE

■ ■ ■ ■ ■

• Empowerment
• Security
• Self-esteem
• Meaning

● ● ● ● ●

Shock
and Denial

• Avoidance
• Confusion
• Fear
• Numbness
• Blame

Acceptance

• Exploring options
• A new plan in place

Anger

• Frustration
• Anxiety
• Irritation
• Embarrassment
• Shame

Dialogue and
Bargaining

• Reaching out to others
• Desire to tell one's story
• Struggle to find meaning for what has happened

Depression and
Detachment

• Overwhelmed
• Blahs
• Lack of energy
• Helplessness

The new thinking is that there is **no series of steps to be completed** in the grieving process. Instead the chart can look more like this:

How You'd Think
Grief Would Go

How It Really
Goes

Grief is unique to each one of us and it's personal. What makes parental grief different from other grief is that parents try to keep their memories from the past, while letting go of the dreams and goals they had for their child's future. Parents say this isn't a loss you "get over." You have to learn how to navigate through your life with this loss.

Distinguishing Between Grief and Mourning

Merriam-Webster dictionary shows the definition of "grief" as a deep sadness caused especially by someone's death — a noun focusing on the *feelings*. "Mourn" is a verb and means to feel or show great sadness because someone has died — the actions taken. Thus grief is the sadness we feel inside and mourning is how we deal with the sadness.

Dr. Alan Wolfelt says in his article "Grief vs. Mourning:" *"If grief is what we think and feel inside, what is mourning? Mourning is the outward expression of our grief. Mourning is crying, talking about the loss, journaling, sharing memories, and telling stories.*

Other ways to mourn include praying, making things, joining in ceremonies, and participating in support groups. Mourning is how, over time, we begin to heal. It is through active and honest mourning that we reconstruct hope and meaning in our lives." [2]

Spousal Relationships After the Loss of a Child

I've heard many people talk about the agony of not only losing a child, but also losing their spouse during those first years. Luckily that didn't happen to my friend, Sandie Loewenthal. But here's what she told me about how grief affected her and her husband differently.

In the year that Stephanie died (about 23 years ago), 75% - 80% of bereaved parents divorced within the first 3-4 years of the child's death. And the rate is still very high. The reason is because I could be having a good day and my husband's having a horrible day. The next day he's having a good day and I'm having a horrible one. We're never on the same level because everyone grieves differently. Mainly the tough part is that people don't understand. They think that two weeks later you're supposed to be better . . . and you're not. You're not better 30 years later.

Ann-Patrice Foley, LMSW (Licensed Master's Social Worker) in her article "Grief and gender... is there a difference?" agrees with Sandie. She says: *"Parental bereavement can place stress on a marital or parental relationship. Suffering a common loss may not draw partners together. It is in recognizing, understanding, validating, and allowing the differences — where healing of the relationship can occur."* [3]

Here's Another Version of "How Grief Can Affect a Marriage" – By Pat Schwiebert, R.N. [4]

Each person grieves in his or her own unique way. This is true even for two parents who are grieving the loss of the same child. It is not uncommon, however, for one partner to evaluate the other partner's grieving process based on his or her own style of grieving. He wants her to behave just like he does, and vice versa. If she cries, she thinks he should cry. If he doesn't want to talk he thinks she shouldn't need to talk either.

Behind this pressure to conform is the subtle assumption that one partner's grief will be validated by the behavior of the other partner. In truth, however, how one will most naturally respond to grief, as a man or as a woman, is conditioned by other factors.

Dealing with the grief factor in a relationship is like driving a car with only one cylinder working. Because grief is both physically and emotionally exhausting some people admit they just don't have the energy to care enough to make their marriage work. That doesn't mean the love is gone, only the energy. But know this as grieving partners: Your marriage not only can survive but thrive if both of you are willing to make your relationship a priority during this difficult time.

Example of Spouses Surviving Grief Well

I interviewed Jill Vasquez who lost her daughter, Annalisa, after only 15 days of life. Her daughter was born at 24 weeks (1 pound, 9 ounces) with a hole in her heart. Medication was given to correct that condition, but it caused a hole in her intestine. After surgery there were complications and her little body just couldn't cope anymore. Jill and her family had the chance to spend those 15 precious days with Annalisa and the bond will endure for a lifetime. Here's what she said about how her husband, Andrew, handled it:

> My husband took her death extremely hard. He expressed a lot of anger and frustration and stuff. He is the Dad — the Protector — yet he could not protect her. And that is what he finally came to terms with — that he could NOT protector her from dying. But his healing is different from most males, I think. He would listen to music all night, even though he would cry with it, he would listen to music. But it would bring me down to listen to it, so I went away from it and would do other things.
>
> Andrew used to drive to Santa Fe (60 miles away) every day for three years. And he drove by the cemetery on his way home and sometimes he would stop and sit by her grave for hours. I had no clue. He'd just sit there and talk to her. Now nine years later we don't visit her gravesite as much anymore or do the decorations like fake flowers and pinwheels like we used to. But that's because we know she's not there — that she's with us. We still have lots of photos of Annalisa in our home and in our hearts, and we also remember her with

butterflies. So I always have butterfly earrings or something with butterflies on it close by.

About Grief and Children

Sometimes we forget that children grieve too. When talking with children about death keep in mind that honesty, compassion and love are essential components of the conversation.

Here are some simple steps you can take to help the child understand and cope with the loss: [5]

- Talk with the child in language he or she can understand. Then let the child explain back to you what he/she thinks you said. Very young children may not have words for their grief and may express their grief easier through drawings or their behavior. Reassure them about the cause of death.

- Encourage children to ask questions and listen carefully, so you can answer what they are asking about, not what they are not.

- Share your own feelings with children and encourage them to be open about theirs. Remember you are a role model for them on how to handle grief.

- Maintain normal routines as much as possible. Children crave and are reassured by structure and repetition.

- Recognize that each child will grieve differently depending on their own level, how close they were to the child who died and the influence of what is going on around them.

- Help the child commemorate the life of the child who died. Sharing memories, creative writing, telling stories, and other activities provide healthy outlets for grief and can be ways to maintain happy memories.

━━━━━━━➤➤➤╫◄◄◄━━━━━━━

Online Support for Bereaved Parents

Here are five well-respected websites which offer online support:

Grief Net (https://griefnet.org) is an on-line community of the bereaved helping the bereaved since 1994. Over 55 **e-mail support groups** provide virtual time discussions of specific losses, such a loss of a parent, loss of a child, loss due to suicide, military losses, etc. GriefNet is a non-profit organization.

Kid Said (www.kidsaid.com) offers **email grief support for kids** — run by GriefNet.org. KidSaid *"is a safe place for kids to help each other deal with grief and loss. It's a* *place to deal with feelings in our e-mail support group, to share and view artwork and stories, and for parents and kids to ask questions and find answers."*

Heal Grief (www.healgrief.org) is a 501(c)3 web-based organization, providing community, support and connections to the bereaved. *"Serving bereaved individuals with a virtual platform designed to aid and transition one's grief into a healthy grief recovery."*

Grief Haven (www.griefHaven.org) is operated by The Erika Whitmore Godwin Foundation — a nonprofit 501(c)3. *"We are parents who are traveling this unwanted path of grieving the loss of our children. None of us want to be here. Whether your child was with you for fifteen minutes or 50 years, the end result is the same. Your beloved child is gone, and now you are left to pick up the pieces and go on. We are here to show you some of the ways, to let you know that you are never alone, and, if you will allow, to walk with you as you traverse this path."*

Open To Hope (www.OpenToHope.com) - giving a voice to grief and recovery. Open to Hope Foundation® is a non-profit foundation with the mission of helping people find hope after loss. It is an online website where people can share inspirational stories of loss and love. They encourage visitors to read, listen and share their stories of hope and compassion. They provide articles, books, and an online community *"to help people deal with difficult losses and continue to live happy, meaningful lives while working through grief."* There is a special section for grieving the loss of a child.

(A Summary)
The Mourner's Bill of Rights
by Alan D. Wolfelt, Ph.D.[6]

You have the right to experience your own unique
grief.

You have the right to talk about your grief.

You have the right to feel a multitude of emotions.

You have the right to be tolerant of your physical
and emotional limits.

You have the right to experience "grief bursts."

You have the right to make use of ritual.

You have the right to embrace your spirituality.

You have the right to search for meaning.

You have the right to treasure your memories.

You have the right to move toward your grief and
heal.

Footnotes:

[1] Five Stages of Grief by Elisabeth Kübler-Ross in her *On Death and Dying* (1969) — originally intended to explain steps that terminally ill patients go through, but generally broadened to include other types of loss.

[2] The "Grief vs. Mourning" quote by Dr. Wolfelt is reprinted with his permission. See his entire article at https://www.centerforloss.com/grief/

[3] This quote on grief and gender by Ann-Patrice Foley, LMSW, is a small fragment from her article entitled: "**This is not a club you would join . . .**" which is available to you with the author's written permission as Appendix i at the end of this book.

[4] How Grief Can Affect a Marriage by Pat Schwiebert, R.N. reprinted in part here with written permission of the author. You may read the entire article online at: https://www.griefwatch.com/how-grief-can-affect-a-marriage. Also see the article https://www.griefwatch.com/men-and-grief.

[5] http://www.caringinfo.org/files/public/brochures/child_cope_death.pdf
and http://www.handonline.org/parents/siblings.html

[6] The Mourner's Bill of Rights - by Alan D. Wolfelt, Ph.D. referenced here with his written permission. See Appendix ii for the complete version of his Mourner's Bill of Rights. And for more information, visit www.centerforloss.com.

Other Resources:

Book: *Healing a parents grieving heart* by Alan D. Wolfelt, Ph.D., available through his www.centerforloss.com website or at Amazon.com.

Article: Visit http://nationalshare.org/children/ for an excellent article about supporting bereaved children — written by Share's former Executive Director, Cathi Lammert, R.N.

Chapter 3

Interacting with Family and Friends

From the Viewpoint of the Bereaved Parent

I've seen and heard lots of ideas about what family and friends might say to bereaved parents, and some of those ideas are here in this chapter. But I've seen very little about what a bereaved parent might say to family and friends — EXCEPT for what Jennifer Dugan wrote on a memorial website page she created about her daughter, Megan. I met Jennifer about a month after Megan died suddenly at 21 months for no apparent reason (SUDS — Sudden Unexplained Death Syndrome). Jennifer dispels some "myths" about what people should do or say to a grieving parent.[1] Here is part of Megan's Story . . .

For those who want to help, please don't forget her. Don't be afraid to talk about her because you think it will upset us. Don't pretend she didn't exist or that we need to not remember her in order to move on. If you have a great story to tell us about her, please share. If you have a picture to show us, let us see it. Don't take down her pictures or not say her name. Megan is a beautiful name which we hope to hear in the name of grandchildren someday.

We love to hear about her. We love to talk about her. We love to share stories and look at pictures. We love to know her life had meaning and purpose. We love to know that people will miss her.

If you have children, hug them tight. When they are driving you nuts which did happen a time or two for us... remember that you are so blessed to have your children. If they want you to stop what you are doing to play on the floor, do it. Take a sick day at work and go to the zoo or the park. Don't worry about the small stuff because you will cherish every moment you have with them if they are ever taken.

Do something in memory of Megan. Whether it be plant a tree or garden or help a child who needs help. Help someone out or do something good and send us a note telling us about it. If we know that Megan's memory is with everyone else, it will help.

Visit us or invite us to something. We need the people who love us around us. Don't be afraid to bring your children or new baby because we want to see them.

When a Child Dies: A Guide for Family and Friends

This guide comes from the caringinfo.org website and defines the steps that friends and family can take to keep the friendship alive.[2] The words are simple, but deep.

Things you can do to support the child's family during this time of sorrow:

Listen. Offer a place of comfort and safety for your friend to express sorrow. You will be offering your friend a huge gift by listening without passing judgment or attempting to fix the pain.

Say the name of the child who died out loud. Grieving parents often find it comforting to hear the name of their child spoken aloud and know that their child is remembered and missed.

Support your friend. It is important to parents and other family members—and to you—that you let them know through words or action that you will be there to help them through this difficult time. Don't let the fear of saying or doing the wrong thing stop you from supporting your friend.

Be patient. Remember grief has no timeline. We visit and revisit all of our losses and grief reactions over an extended period of time.

Reminisce and share stories and memories. Let your friend guide you. For example, "I have such a wonderful memory of your child. Would you like me to share it now or another time?"

Stay away from "shoulds". For example, "You should go out more, try to eat more (or less), go to your place of worship more, read this book, or come over for lunch."

Embrace the silence. The ability to just be present and quiet with your friend can be very comforting during times of sorrow.

What to Say and Not Say

4 of the BEST things to say to someone in grief are:

1) "I am so sorry for your loss."
2) "I wish I had the right words, just know I care."
3) "I don't know how you feel, but I am here to help in any way I can."
4) "You and your loved one will be in my thoughts and prayers"

4 of the WORST things to say to someone in grief are:

1) "He/she is in a better place."
2) "There is a reason for everything."
3) "At least you can have another child."
4) "I know how you feel." (unless you are a bereaved parent also.)

Many of us have said *The Best* and *The Worst*.[3] We didn't mean any harm; in fact, we were trying to comfort. But we just need to say: "I'm so sorry for your loss," listen to them and be present in their grief.

Sometimes Even Best Friends Don't Understand

Here's a story told by Jill Vasquez:

> My best friend and I were pregnant at the
> same time with girls. Her daughter is 11
> days older than Annalisa would have been.
> It was hard because she kind of stopped
> talking to me. She kind of avoided me. We
> would say in the Share group meetings that
> people think we had the plague or
> something. Like they think if they get close
> to you that something is going to happen to
> them, which is ridiculous. I mean you don't
> know who it's going to happen to. And so she
> totally avoided me and when I finally talked
> to her, she said 'I didn't know what to say
> and thought you would be mad because my
> daughter, Sienna, is here'.
>
> I told her 'In a way I can see my daughter
> growing up with Sienna, because they would
> be the same age and everything. I don't want
> you to pull away from me right now. I need
> you close to me right now.' And she kind of
> got a little upset too because after we had
> our daughters of course they were trying for
> another one and I had already gotten
> pregnant again and she had not. She'd ask:
> 'How can you keep popping out babies like
> crazy and I can't have more than one?' And
> I'm like 'Well if you think about it, I'd rather
> have a couple that go full term than have

three that are born preemies. But that is just what I was handed'. So we talk now and then, but it's not the same relationship we used to have.

Footnotes:

[1] Taken from the Memorial website Jennifer created to remember her daughter, Megan. She gave me written permission to include the page in this book, in hopes that it helps others. The full website can be viewed at http://rememberingmegan.weebly.com.

[2] When a Child Dies: A Guide for Family and Friends – Reprinted here with written permission from CaringInfo - a program of the National Hospice and Palliative Care Organization. CaringInfo provides information and support for anyone who is planning ahead, caregiving, living with a serious illness or grieving a loss. http://www.caringinfo.org/files/public/brochures/When_A_ Child_Dies.pdf

[3] To read the original "10 Best & Worst Things to Say to Someone in Grief", visit http://grief.com/10-best-worst-things-to-say-to-someone-in-grief/

Chapter 4

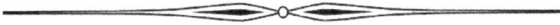

Connecting with a Support Group in Your Area

"I wish I'd done one thing differently.
I wish we'd joined the Compassionate Friends group sooner."
- Sandie Loewenthal

The Compassionate Friends – A Story

A friend of mine, Sandie Loewenthal told me about how she and her husband Mike lost their daughter, Stephanie, when she was just 3 months old. Stephanie had heart problems that surgery just couldn't cure. In her words:

> We had a friend who lost her son about a year and a half before our Stephanie died. Our friend was still going to the Compassionate Friends group when Stephanie died and after about 3 weeks, she called us and said to Mike, 'you and Sandie need to come visit the group with me.' I

didn't want anything to do with it. And Mike kept pushing me to go and I said 'No, I'm not ready.' And I wish I had gone sooner. Groups like that are like a safe haven, because everybody is in the same boat. It wasn't a feeling of relief . . . I felt safe. I felt loved by all those strangers there — from the minute I walked in. The thing is . . . it's like an open wound. The sooner you get help — the sooner you start healing. Life starts taking on some normalcy. Not that it will ever be normal again. But you know, you pull yourself up by your bootstraps and life goes on.

The Compassionate Friends group was a *'godsend'*, she said, and she and Mike remained with the group for several years, taking on leadership and mentorship roles to help new families as they came along. *"As we meet together, we learn from each other through our shared experiences."*

From the Compassionate Friends website - https://www.CompassionateFriends.org:
*"The Compassionate Friends offers more than **660** meeting locations around the country. In small towns and large cities, bereaved parents, siblings, and grandparents meet together to talk, listen, share, and provide each other emotional support after the devastating death of a child. When you attend chapter sessions, you won't find professionals running the meetings and giving advice. We are not therapists and we do not provide counseling. Everyone will be just like you, someone who is going through the natural grieving process."*

National Share – A Story

I mentioned Jill Vasquez and her husband, Andrew, in Chapter 2. Their daughter, Annalisa, was born in October at 24 weeks and died after just 15 days in the NICU. Both parents attended the New Mexico Chapter of National Share, aptly called New Mexico Share. The group meets once a month and they went for a year. After that, so many of the women attending were pregnant again that they actually branched off another group they called Subsequent Choices. The fear with these women is that the loss will happen again. This was especially true with Jill, as the due date for her next child was just a year and two days different from Annalisa's due date. Jill was a nervous wreck until the 24 weeks went by. Her son delivered at 30 weeks; and though he was just 3 pounds, 4 ounces, he was healthy and has grown to be a typical energetic child.

The Rewarding Part - Eight years later, Jill has this to say:

> Several times each year, the Share coordinator asks us to come and attend a meeting because a newly bereaved couple is going to be there. And now we can go and meet the people who are raw. We tell them our story and usually most of the group is just nodding their heads, because they have all been through the same feelings and situations. And it helps the new ones to hear

— You had those feeling too? — and we go Yeah we did. This is where it has brought us today. You're okay. With a different special bond that no one else can feel. And it's really rewarding for us to help people go through that process. And they'd be like thank you so much for being there and being so understanding — advising them as to what can help.

From National Share's website - http://nationalshare.org/: *"Share's mission is to serve those whose lives are touched by the tragic death of a baby through pregnancy loss, stillbirth or in the first few months of life. We strive to set a standard of personalized perinatal bereavement care through a lifetime of support, hope and healing - one family at a time."* There are currently over 75 Share Chapters in 29 states.

Other Well-Established Support Groups for Bereaved Parents

Bereaved Parents of the USA —

http://bereavedparentsusa.org/
"A national non-profit self-help group that offers support, understanding, compassion and hope especially to the newly bereaved — be they bereaved parents, grandparents or siblings struggling to rebuild their lives after the death of their children, grandchildren or siblings." There are currently face-to-face support chapters in 34 states and

their national website has many resources for dealing with grief.

MISS Foundation — http://www.missfoundation.org/
A non-profit 501(c)3 international organization providing immediate and ongoing support to grieving families, helping them to empower themselves by proactive community involvement and volunteerism, and reducing infant and toddler death through research and education. There are currently MISS Foundation Chapters in 15 states and the website has an abundance of resources for dealing with grief.

The Value of a Support Group

Pros . . .
From Jane Fleming, MPM Grief Support Specialist at Providence Hospice of Seattle, WA says:

> I coordinate the bereavement program for the Stepping Stones Palliative Care Program at Providence Hospice of Seattle. In 2010, I offered a support group for three couples who had each lost a baby in the previous twelve months.
>
> Meeting with other parents in a supportive environment has been integral in the work of healing. Cate sums it up for everyone with the sentiment — 'I am so grateful that I can take these two hours every month to just

talk about Tommy — my life is so busy now with baby Rose, this is a place I can talk about losing him and missing him and everyone gets it'.

What to Watch For . . .

Though support groups help a lot of parents, they are not for everyone. And sometimes parents stay too long, continue reliving the pain and don't heal. It's important for those attending to realize when it might be time to step away. Here's what Jill Vasquez has to say:

> After the first year we didn't go to the Share group so often because those same feelings would come up again — they'd resurface — and they weren't going away and we weren't moving forward. We would hear the stories and then feel bad because our relationship was so tight as a couple.

She and her husband stepped away and are able to come back every now and again to help others, as they mentioned in "The Rewarding Part" above.

Footnote:

Jane Fleming's quote in the "Pros" section above is just a small part of an article you can read online through this link: http://www.nhpco.org/sites/default/files/public/ChiPPS/ChiPPS_Issue23_May-2011.pdf

Chapter 5

Creating an Online Memorial for Your Child

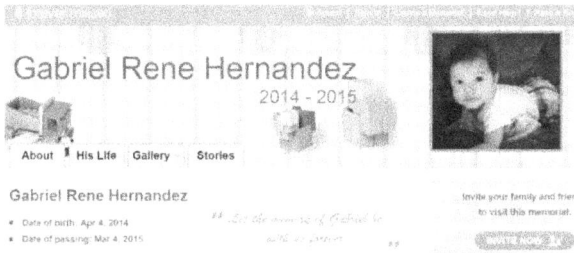

Share the memory of your child with friends and family with an online webpage.

By creating a website in memory of your child, you can help yourself and your family heal. There are a number of online sites to memorialize a person and they have different features. If the parents aren't able to set up a site, a friend or relative could make it happen — with the family's permission.

As you know, what is available online today will be different by tomorrow. But the ideas stated here will give you a guideline of options you can look for in a Memorial website or webpage offering.

Major Types of Online Memorial Pages

- A regular website you make yourself, which tells everyone what you want them to know about your child. It is meant to be informative and does not allow for anyone else to add to it. Some of these are free and some are not.

- An online Memorial Website where you create a "page" for your loved one within the existing website and friends and family can contribute to it with their stories, photos and videos. Some of these "pages" are free and some are not.

- You could memorialize a Facebook page if your child had one. The major downside is that only "friends" of that page can see it. No one else can see it and it is not searchable within Facebook.

CAUTION — Beware of Identity Theft Possibilities
Children of any age (both alive and deceased) can become easy victims of identity theft. Be careful of how much personal information you share on the internet. Of course, a regular website will be public, and most Memorial Webpages give you the option of whether to make the webpage public or private (password protected). Facebook is private to "friends" only.

Create a Regular Website

You may want to create a regular website, where you have total control over the content. If you just want to create a memorial yourself and aren't looking for additional stories and photos from friends, this may be for you. There are number of companies offering free websites. One I'm familiar with is Weebly.com

Weebly.com offers a FREE website with limited features that will work for a Memorial Tribute to your child. It offers a drag and drop builder, free hosting and unlimited pages. Free pages have a storage limit of 500MB. Chat and Email support are available during the process of construction. You have a choice of templates.

For an example, a customer of mine used Weebly.com to create a memorial website for her 20-month old daughter, Megan. Visit http://rememberingmegan.weebly.com to see what can be done with the available features.

Another website is **Wix.com**. Their website says the Wix website builder has everything you need to create a fully personalized, high-quality free website. I couldn't find out much information though without just getting started — which I didn't want to do. So by all means, check it out. They have a good name and millions of users worldwide.

Utilize a Memorial Website – My Top 6 Picks

If you prefer to have the basic framework already done for you, there are a number of sites available designed as Memorial Websites. They will include design features specifically intended as a memorial site and include pages already set up for "stories" and "photo gallery" and "tributes". That makes it really easy to upload the information into the right place.

Here are my top six picks — going from "best" to "not so much." All allow stories, comments and/or tributes to be added to the page by friends and family.

If you prefer to see a CHART comparing the features of the six websites, see Appendix iii at the end of this book.

ForeverMissed.com

Overview: This is a very easy-to-use site with a very pleasant look and feel to the pages.

Choice of Templates: Yes

Simple URL: Yes (www.forevermissed.com/first-last/)

SHARE button to invite family and friends to the site: Yes

Number of pages: 4

Number photos: 3

Number of videos: none

Allows the site to be either public or private: Yes

Has Advertising on its pages: No

Site Owners home state: New York

Pricing: Basic described above is FREE.

Upgrade: $34.95/year includes unlimited photos and videos

Lifetime: $74.95

Never-Gone.com

Overview: This site has a pleasant look and feel to the pages.

Choice of Templates: Yes

Simple URL: Yes, custom

SHARE button to invite family and friends to the site: Yes

Number of pages: 7

Number photos: No limit

Number of videos: No limit

Allows the site to be either public or private: Yes

Has Advertising on its pages: No (except for 1 small one asking if the viewer wants to create a webpage)

Site Owners home state: Florida, I believe

Pricing: FREE — Never-Gone.com says it "is now the only **fully featured 100% free forever** online memorial website on the Internet." **They will also create a tribute video free of charge** which can be used for the service or for personal use.

iLasting.com

Overview: This is a very pleasant looking site

Choice of Templates: Yes

Simple URL: Yes (http://www.ilasting.com/firstlast.php)

SHARE button to invite family and friends to the site: Yes

Number of pages: 7

Number photos: 5

Number of videos: None

Allows stories and comments from visitors: Limit of 5 stories on Free page

Allows the site to be either public or private: Yes

Has Advertising on its pages: No

Site Owners home state: California

Pricing: Basic described above is FREE.

Upgrade: $49/year includes up to 100 photos, 5 videos, unlimited stories, a Timeline and a Donation-to-charity Page

Lifetime: $99.00

Memorialwebsites.Legacy.com

Overview: Very pleasant look and feel to the pages

Choice of Templates: Yes

Simple URL: Yes

(http://memorialwebsites.legacy.com/firstlast/homepage.aspx)

SHARE button to invite family and friends to the site: Yes

Number of pages: 8

Number photos: 150

Number of videos: 30 audio or video

Allows the site to be either public or private: Yes

Has Advertising on its pages: No

Site Owners home state: Illinois

Pricing: Basic described above is FREE for 14 days. After that, the page is archived. Can be sponsored anytime and will be visible for 1 year.

Sponsorship: $49 plus $19/year

GoneTooSoon.org

Overview: Site offers all-around bereavement services, and the main page is a bit cluttered, as it includes celebrity memorials as well. Design for individual memorial not very pleasant.

Choice of Templates: Yes — choice of 3

Simple URL: Yes (http://www.gonetoosoon.org/memorials/first-last)

SHARE button to invite family and friends to the site: No

Number of pages: 1

Number photos: unlimited

Number of videos: 1

Allows the site to be either public r private: Yes

Has Advertising on its pages: YES

Site Owners home state: United Kingdom

Pricing: Basic described above is FREE.

Upgrade: 3 pounds/month (= about $4.50) includes 12 themes and 3 videos

Lifetime: none

Tributes.com

Overview: Home page has a cluttered look to it as it includes celebrity memorials. Individual pages are also very busy, though I guess they get the job done. Not very user friendly.

Choice of Templates: only in Upgrade

Simple URL: No

SHARE button to invite family and friends to the site: Yes

Number of pages: 3

Number photos: none, except unlimited in Upgrade

Number of videos: none, except unlimited in Upgrade

Allows the site to be either public or private: I don't think so, site doesn't say.

Has Advertising on its pages: YES

Site Owners home state: Illinois

Pricing: Basic: NOT FREE — unless you choose to use the Fundraising-for-the-Family feature. Then all the features are free. They also offer an Obituary notice only option for $20, which includes one photo.

Upgrade: $50/lifetime includes no limit on photos and video uploads and a choice of themes.

Memorialize a Facebook page

A Facebook account can now be "Memorialized" when a person dies. A family member or 'friend' can request that an account be memorialized upon production of proof of death. When the account is memorialized, Facebook removes sensitive information such as contact information and status updates, but still enables friends and family to leave posts on the profile wall in remembrance. A Memorialized Facebook page is only visible to existing "friends". No one else can see it.

Chapter 6

Handling Milestone Dates and Holidays

Grief and the Holidays
From Grief.com[1]

Holidays are time spent with loved ones" was imprinted on our psyche from a young age. Holidays mark the passage of time in our lives. They are part of the milestones we share with each other and they generally represent time spent with family. They bring meaning to certain days and we bring much meaning back to them.

But since holidays are for being with those we love the most, how on earth can anyone be expected to cope with them when a loved one has died? For many people, this is the hardest part of grieving, when we miss our loved ones even more than usual. How can you celebrate togetherness when there is none?

When you have lost someone special, your world loses its celebratory qualities. Holidays only magnify the loss. The sadness feels sadder and the loneliness goes deeper. The need for support may be the greatest during the holidays. Pretending you don't hurt and or it is not a harder time of the year is just not the truth for you. You can and will get through the holidays. Rather than avoiding the feelings of grief, lean into them. It is not the grief you want to avoid; it is the pain. Grief is the way out of the pain. There are a number of ways to incorporate your loved one and your loss into the holidays.

Ways to Cope

Mentally —

Here are a few ideas from a variety of people who've lost loved ones and found ways that helped them cope with their grief during the holidays.[2]

Acknowledge that the holidays will be different and they will be tough.

Give yourself permission to change your usual holiday traditions. Decide which ones you want to keep and which ones you want to change. No apologies to others needed.

Decide where you want to spend the holidays — you may want to switch up the location, or it may be of comfort to keep it the same. Either way, make a conscious decision about location.

Don't send holiday cards this year if it is too sad or overwhelming and don't feel guilty about not sending them.

Remember that not everyone will be grieving the same way you are grieving.

Remember that the way others will want to spend the holiday may not match how you want to spend the holiday.

Do allow others to help. We all need a little help sometimes and it will let both you and the person helping feel better.

At your holiday event, ask for a few moments to be spent remembering your child. Share a favorite story and ask others to tell their favorite story too.

Have a Plan A and a Plan B — Plan A is you go to the Thanksgiving, Christmas Day or Christmas Eve dinner with family and friends. If it doesn't feel right, have your Plan B ready. Plan B may be a movie you both liked or a photo album to look through or a special place you went to together. Many people find that when they have Plan B in place, just knowing it is there is enough.

Don't get trapped. When you go to holiday events, drive

yourself so you can leave if it gets to be too much.

For some, staying involved with the holidays is a symbol of life continuing. If this is you, be sure to prioritize and don't overcommit. If the holidays are filled with parties, dinners, and events, save your energy for the most important ones and skip the rest.

Cancel the holiday all together. Yes, you can cancel the holiday. If you are going through the motions and feeling nothing, cancel it. Take a year off. The holiday will come around again.

If you do skip the holidays though, make a plan. Decide if you will still see friends or family, go see a new movie, or make another plan.

Physically —

Especially during the holidays, it may help to externalize the loss a bit. See if you can do something or create something physical in memory of your child.

Create a new tradition in memory of your child.

Buy a gift you would have given to your loved one and donate it to a local charity.

Pick a few special items that belonged to your loved one and gift them to friends or family who will appreciate them.

Create a Memorial Website for your child. You can tell a story and read comments and stories left by friends and family. *(see chapter 5 for details)*

Light a candle in memory of your child in your home or in your place of worship.

Talk to kids about the holidays — it can be confusing for kids that the holidays can be both happy and sad after a death. Let them know it is okay to enjoy the holiday, and it is okay to be sad.

▬►►▪◄◄▬

A Novel Approach

Set aside a designated time each day or each week to grieve.

(This may strike you as really strange,
but for some people it may help give them a little more
control over their emotions.)

The Huffington Post had an article in 2013 about "9 Scientifically-Backed Ways to Stop Worrying" which, I think, might be applied to grieving. Not to "stop" grieving, but to help keep grieving from consuming so much of your time — like "worry" does for some people. Here's what they said, except I substituted their word "worry" with the word "grieve".[3]

Set aside a designated "grieve time."

Instead of grieving all day, every day, **designate a 30-minute period of time** where you can think about your problems (your grief, your child, how you're coping with the loss). Penn State researchers found in a 2011 study that a four-step stimulus control program could help seriously grieving people take control of their grief.

Step one: Identify the object of grief.

Step two: Come up with a time and place to think about said grief.

Step three: If you catch yourself grieving at a time other than your designated grief time, you must make a point to think of something else.

Step four: Use your "grieve time" productively by thinking of solutions to the grief (positive steps you can take to work through the grief).

Remembering — Time and Again

**The Teddy Bear Legacy —
an alternative to flowers on the grave**

I talked about the Teddy Bear Legacy in Chapter 1 — where a link in the obituary lets friends and family send cuddly teddy bears to children in the hospital — in your child's name.

But there is a second way the Teddy Bear Legacy can help families cope with the grief. I think this is a modern version of putting flowers on a grave, but where the "flowers" (in this case the teddy bears) "do an extra good" because they comfort children who are going through their own struggles in the hospital. And the person who donates feels better because they know the bears are helping other children.

Parents and family members can continue to donate teddy bears in the name of their child anytime. It can be for your child's birthday, death anniversary or as a new tradition during the holidays. It could be a teddy bear a month for the first year — whatever helps. The links on the www.TeddyBearLegacy.com website remain active for years and years and years, so teddy bear donations can be made anytime.

The first Teddy Bear Legacy family occurred in 2010 and the maternal grandmother still comes back to the website each year and donates four or five teddy bears in her grandson's name. The bears still get sent to the same children's hospital in Washington, DC that they did when we started. The hospital loves the comfort the bears gives the children who receive them and the grandmother has a chance to mourn and put "fresh flowers" on her grandson's grave.

Any parent, family member or friend can register for the Teddy Bear Legacy if one wasn't set up when the child died. Keep in mind that someone in the family will need to let other people know about it and tell them the website name (www.TeddyBearLegacy.com) so they can go there to purchase bears in the child's name. If you have questions, please contact me.

Resources:

[1] Grief and the Holidays — Visit the website (http://grief.com) for many other suggestions on how to cope with grief

[2] http://www.whatsyourgrief.com/64-tips-grief-at-the-holidays/

[3] http://www.huffingtonpost.com/2013/10/01/stop-worrying-anxiety-cycle_n_4002914.htm

This is not a club you would join...

By Ann-Patrice Foley, LMSW

These were the words of my preceptor, a number of years ago, during my internship at Angela Hospice in Livonia, Michigan.

These words have stuck with me. As I continue in her legacy and become increasingly involved with parents whose child or children have died, I remember these words: "This is not a club you would join."

"But," I often think, "without having chosen to, so many parents are in the club anyway, so what now?"

When we lose our grandparents or our parents, we lose a piece of our past. We can be sad and grieve such a loss, but we expect it to happen. When we lose our spouse, partner, sibling or close friend, we lose a piece of our present. From the time we understand death, and the finality of it, we know that these losses are a real possibility. However, when we lose a child, we lose our future.

This is not the kind of loss we "expect" to happen. Oh, we know it happens. We hear about it. Pregnant moms miscarry or have still-born babies. Babies have abnormalities, sometimes genetic, sometimes not.

Children get sick. Children have accidents. Children are in accidents. Children are killed. Children take their lives.

But this happens to others. God forbid. Not us, right?

Your child has died. Now what? What is a parent to do?

Parents can spend a life-time trying to make sense of this type of loss. Many times, in the course of working with parents whose child is dying (or has died) I have heard parents say, "I'm trying to make sense out of a senseless situation; I just can't wrap my head around it."

While the death of any loved one, particularly a child, will always be a unique and highly individual experience, there are commonalities in the grief process. The grief process for bereaved parents is both intense and lengthy. It is critical to recognize the multiple facets and layers of parental grief that make it different from other kinds of grief. Literature that states that "normal grief lasts six months to one year," is found to be inadequate and false when applied to parental grief. Parents struggle to retain and preserve memories from the past, while letting go of the dreams and goals for the future with their child. Parents tell us and remind us... this isn't a loss you "get over." You have to learn how to navigate through your life with this loss.

So how long does this grief last?

Our logic tells us that grief will decline steadily over time. In reality, the experience is not so much a healing as a gradual acceptance of a pain that fluctuates in intensity and changes in complexity over time, but does not disappear. Parents tell us that, in most cases, such grief may be more intense after one year has passed. They say there are many factors that make this a reality. During the first year, they have their "guard up." Parents often try to mentally prepare for their experiences without their child. The child's first birthday, holidays, back to school, the anniversary of the death. Then, as time continues, parents state they let their "guard" down a little, and their family and friends are less vigilant, too. Parents voice, "It has been 'that much longer' since I held my child, felt my child, heard my child." They miss their child's scent, and long for anything that will bring back those memories.

The extended family and friends, who may have been acutely aware during the first year of grief and were often protective of the parents and sensitive to their loss, often transition to a new message to the bereaved parents. In verbal or non-verbal ways, these well-meaning loved ones convey that it is now time to move on, and make changes that bereaved parents are often not ready to make.

Parents state that they are fearful that people will forget their child. They express the fear that even as parents, they too will forget certain aspects of their precious child. They are afraid of forgetting some of the details and the memories that are important to them. Numerous parents tell me they thought they were going crazy, because the second year hurt more not less. Additionally, if the parents become pregnant with a new child, the community that serves them often believes the parents should not continue to feel sad. Family, friends, and co-workers do not understand why parents continue to grieve about a child who has died, since they now have a new child to look forward to. People often assume that the arrival of a new child will take away the pain of the child who died. Parents repeatedly report that this is not their truth.

So how long does parental grief last? Talk to any parent, of any age, who has had a child die. I recently met a woman in her nineties, who was dying in our Angela Hospice Care Center, and she told me that she had two children predecease her. One who died at childbirth; one died when the child was a teenager.

I asked her this question: "How long did your grief last?"

She replied without hesitation..."It still exists."

She went on to explain, "There are good days and there are bad."

So the answer to the question? It lasts as long as it lasts.

Grief and gender...is there a difference?

Parental bereavement can place stress on a marital or parental relationship. Suffering a common loss may not draw partners together. Each parent has experienced a severe dismemberment of self. They may feel incapacitated and unable to help each other or fulfill parental roles. Mothers and fathers tend to grieve differently, and are often out of sync with one another in their grief. There is no "right" or "wrong" way to grieve. It is important to learn about and recognize some of the gender differences, so they can be dealt with—allowing each parent to have a better understanding of themselves and each other. It is in recognizing, understanding, validating, and allowing the differences—where healing of the parental relationship can occur.

Standing in the presence of grief.

So how do we help grieving parents? My suggestion is to listen. It is as simple, and as complex, as that.

Listen. Listen. Listen. Stand in the presence of their grief. For however long it takes. Don't put parameters and time-frames to their grief. Be still. Don't be quick to try to "fix" them.

The parents are the ones to teach us. Assume nothing. Let them tell you what they are experiencing, and what they need. Normalize their feelings, thoughts, emotions and concerns. Validate them and invite them to keep coming back. Create a safe place for them to process grief. Allow them to tell their story, over and over if need be. It is often in the telling and retelling of their story that healing takes place. Listen as they relive memories. In an individual, couple, family, or group therapy setting, let them know they are not alone in their thinking and feeling.

Remind them to be gentle on themselves, as they continue on their grief journey. Assist them in creating a "back up plan" for themselves, when life is overwhelming and becomes too much to handle. Give them permission to do things differently. It is important to allow grieving parents to share their experience, strength, and hope. Stand in the presence of their grief.

Turning pain into passion...

So, the members of this club... What can they teach us? I'll tell you what I've seen...

Parents change after going through the death of a child in deep and powerful ways. Bereaved parents are compelled to change what they do, how they live...into something meaningful and genuine. I have discovered that many bereaved parents turn their pain into passion. They are transformed individuals, as a result of their child and their experience. Bereaved parents advocate for research. They raise funds and awareness, to find cures for disease and illnesses. They help create legislative change. They support and promote causes. They cannot be superficial. They help other parents and families, and are deeply compassionate and empathetic people. They have riches and values. There is much they can teach us.

This article is reprinted in its entirety with written permission of the author.

http://www.nhpco.org/sites/default/files/public/ChiPP S/ChiPPS_Issue23_May-2011.pdf

The Mourner's Bill of Rights

By Alan D. Wolfelt, Ph.D., C.T.

Though you should reach out to others as you do the work of mourning, you should not feel obligated to accept the unhelpful responses you may receive from some people. You are the one who is grieving, and as such, you have certain "rights" no one should try to take away from you.

The following list is intended both to empower you to heal and to decide how others can and cannot help. This is not to discourage you from reaching out to others for help, but rather to assist you in distinguishing useful responses from hurtful ones.

1. You have the right to experience your own unique grief. No one else will grieve in the exact same way you do. So, when you turn to others for help, don't allow them to tell you what you should or should not be feeling.

2. You have the right to talk about your grief. Talking about your grief will help you heal. Seek out others who will allow you to talk as much as you want about your grief. If at times you do not feel like talking, you also have the right to be silent.

3. You have the right to feel a multitude of emotions. Confusion, disorientation, fear, guilt, and relief are just a few of the emotions you might feel as part of your grief journey. Others may try to tell you that feeling angry, for example, is wrong. Don't take these judgmental responses to heart. Instead, find listeners who will accept your feelings without conditions.

4. You have the right to be tolerant of your physical and emotional limits. Your feelings of loss and sadness will probably leave you feeling fatigued. Respect what your body and mind are telling you. Get daily rest. Eat balanced meals. And don't allow others to push you into doing things you don't feel ready to do.

5. You have the right to experience "griefbursts". Sometimes, out of nowhere, a powerful surge of grief may overcome you. This can be frightening, but it is normal and natural. Find someone who understands and will let you talk it out.

6. You have the right to make use of ritual. The funeral ritual does more than acknowledge the death of someone loved. It helps provide you with the support of caring people. More importantly, the funeral is a way for you to mourn. If others tell you the funeral or other healing rituals such as these are silly or unnecessary, don't listen.

7. You have the right to embrace your spirituality. If faith is a part of your life, express it in ways that seem appropriate to you. Allow yourself to be around people who understand and support your religious beliefs. If you feel

angry at God, find someone to talk with who won't be critical of your feelings of hurt and abandonment.

8. You have the right to search for meaning. You may find yourself asking, "Why did he or she die? Why this way? Why now?" Some of your questions may have answers, but some may not. And watch out for the clichéd responses some people may give you. Comments like, "It was God's will" or "Think of what you have to be thankful for" are not helpful and you do not have to accept them.

9. You have the right to treasure your memories. Memories are one of the best legacies that exist after the death of someone loved. You will always remember. Instead of ignoring your memories, find others with whom you can share them.

10. You have the right to move toward your grief and heal. Reconciling your grief will not happen quickly. Remember, grief is a process, not an event. Be patient and tolerant with yourself and avoid people who are impatient and intolerant with you. Neither you nor those around you must forget that the death of someone loved changes your life forever.

———————◇◇——◇◇———————

Reprinted in its entirety with written permission of the author. Visit his website, www.centerforloss.com for more information.

My Top Six Picks for Online Memorial Websites - Comparison of Features

My Rating	Website	Cost-FREE?	Feel/Look of page	Choice of Themes	# photos incl.	# videos incl.	Ads?	Public or Private Options	Simple URL?	# pages	Upgrade Plan	# photos incl.	# videos incl.	Lifetime Plan	USA?	Notes
1	ForeverMissed.com	yes	Very Pleasant	yes	3	0	no	yes	yes	4	$34.95/yr	no limit	no limit	$74.95 once	NY	
2	Never-Gone.com	yes	Very Pleasant	yes	no limit	no limit	no	yes	yes	7	N/A	-	-	no	FL?	**Totally Free** - Will create tribute video free
3	iLasting.com	yes	Pleasant	yes	5	no	no	yes	yes	7	$49.00/yr	100	5	$99	CA	
4	Memorialwebsites.Legacy.com	yes for 14 days	Pleasant	yes	150	30	no	yes	yes	8	$49 + $19/yr = pricey	?	?	no	IL	After 14 days page is archived. Can be sponsored any time & be visible for 1yr.
5	GoneTooSoon.org	yes	Pleasant- offers all around bereavement	3	See Upgrade		yes	?	yes	1	3.0 pnds/mo. - = about $4.50	?	3	no	UK	
6	Tributes.com Called "online obituary" - not "memorial site"	**no-** unless fund raising feature used	Cluttered - includes celebrity deaths				yes		no	3	$50 once for lifetime	no limit	no limit	$50 once for lifetime	IL	**only site offering fundraising opp for the family's needs** and Offers a Death Notice Only for $20

About the Author

Why this Book?

In 2008 I created a gift-giving website called MamaBearsPlace.com and happily sold cuddly "pairs of teddy bears" to my customers. One bear goes to their friend or loved one and the twin bear is sent to a child in the hospital. Each bear is shipped with a little tag telling about the twin bear going to comfort the other person — so it is a gift with a benefit that makes both the gift-giver and the recipient feel better — let alone helping the child in the hospital.

Then in 2010 I received an email from a woman in Washington, DC who had just lost her son, James, who was stillborn the week before. I was stunned, but read on. She told me that she was saddened from watching the flowers that people sent her die a little every day and wanted to know if I could arrange for her family and friends to order teddy bears instead, that could all be sent to children in the hospital in DC in the name of her son. I wept. It was such a simple idea, yet so filled with emotion and benefits for so many. It was something her family and friends could do to feel better by helping others in the name of her son.

Of course I said "yes" and set up the details needed on my website. The parents included a link to the website in their son's obituary and over the next several months, more than

50 teddy bears were donated to the children in James' name. The family was so grateful for having this "outlet for coping with grief" that they included a thank you to me in their Christmas letter and sent me a copy.

Last year I decided it was time for the Teddy Bear Legacy to have its own website, so I built one and called it — appropriately — www.TeddyBearLegacy.com, with a tagline of "helping families cope with grief."

I am not a medical doctor, psychologist or social worker. You won't see any initials after my name. So I can't tell you how to get through the process of grieving. But I can share with you what I've learned from years of conversations with grieving parents and from reading the data from well-established social workers and experts in the field. The focus of this book is on the THINGS YOU CAN DO on your journey to survive the loss. I hope it helps.

Brief Bio

I'm a mid-westerner at heart. I was born in Colorado, but grew up in the suburbs of Chicago. My husband and I moved to Atlanta, back to Chicago, over to New Jersey and then to Albuquerque, New Mexico. I love it here in New Mexico. Gorgeous skies, mountains, diversity of flowers and trees, good people, and gorgeous weather. Now I'm a New Mexican, having lived here since '75.

I worked for a national food services distributor here in New Mexico for 32 years, in "bid sales" to the schools, prisons, and senior centers — kind of a captive audience and they definitely have to eat. I have a son who lives in Illinois with his lovely wife and three adorable young daughters. A decade ago I developed a voice issue, and though I talk quite a bit, sometimes it isn't very clear, so I prefer communicating via emails and text messages. So when I Skype with the grandkids, they do most of the talking and each time I'm worn out from their energy and all the laughter.

When I retired, I wanted to start a business from my home that I found interesting — and one which included teddy bears. Hence MamaBearsPlace.com was born and was followed by the Teddy Bear Legacy.com. I love these two websites because they provide services which help people and as an entrepreneur, it keeps me learning things every day.

Donna J Luke

Contact Information:
Phone: 505-307-2906 — because of my voice issues, I don't talk on my cell phone much. It sounds like I'm cutting out all the time. So please leave me a voice message, preferably with your email address included, and I'll get back to you. Or you can text me.

Teddy Bear Legacy.com
HELPING FAMILIES COPE WITH GRIEF

MamaBearsPlace.com
Where One Gift warms TWO hearts

www.TeddyBearLegacy.com
Email: donna@teddybearlegacy.com
www.facebook.com/myteddybearlegacy

www.MamaBearsPlace.com
Email: donna@mamabearsplace.com
www.facebook.com/MamaBearsPlace